First published in Great Britain in 2026
by Wayland

© Hodder and Stoughton, 2026

All rights reserved

Credits:
Editors: Julia Bird; Julia Adams
Design and illustrations: Matt Lilly
Cover design: Matt Lilly

HB ISBN 978 1 5263 2977 6
PB ISBN 978 1 5263 2978 3

Printed and bound in Dubai

Picture credits:

Alamy: Album 26b; Chronicle 15b; Dpa picture alliance 9b; Sahil Ghosh 6c; Spencer Grant 7b; David Grossman 13t; Independent Photo Agency Srl 25b; Joma 19br; Newscom 17; Niday Picture Library 13b; RGR Collection 21bl;Theatrepix 27t; Trinity Mirror/Mirrorpix 15tl; Underwood Archives 15cl;
Getty Images: David Buchan/ Variety 21br.
Shutterstock: Olga Besnard 5b; Igor Bulgarin 16; Sam the Leigh 18t; Master1305 15c; MeinPhoto 10b; Oneinchpunch 5t; PeopleImages.com-Yuri A 11c; Anuparn R 22; Dmitry Ruklenko 4b, 23; Runeun2 28;Roman Samborskyi 15tr; Anastasia Thales 9t; Turkey Photo 6b; Alexander Y 27b.
Wikimedia Commons: R Ballard, 1653/PD 20; Library of Congress,Carl von Viechten Estate/PD 19tr; The Metropolitan Museum of Art, NY/PD 21t; Herman Miskin/University of Washington/PD 21bc.

Every effort has been made to clear copyright.
Should there be any inadvertent omission,
please apply to the publisher for rectification

Wayland
An imprint of
Hachette Children's Group
Part of Hodder and Stoughton
Carmelite House
50 Victoria Embankment
London EC4Y 0DZ

An Hachette UK Company
www.hachette.co.uk
www.hachettechildrens.co.uk

The authorised representative in the EEA is Hachette Ireland,
8 Castlecourt Centre, Dublin 15, D15 XTP3,
Ireland (email: info@hbgi.ie)

Contents

4-5
What is dance?

6-7
Did cave people waltz?

8-9
Where do swords dance?

10-11
Can you have two left feet?

12-13
How do you move to the groove?

14-15
When do people flap like a bird?

16-17
Can you kick a can-can?

18-19
What puts the fizz into K-pop?

20-21
What's the point of going *en pointe*?

22-23
When do you dance with your hands?

24-25
How does a fox trot?

26-27
How can dance break all the rules?

28-29
Quick-fire questions

30-31
Glossary / Further discovery

32
Index

What is dance?

Dance is a form of art where people express themselves by moving their bodies. This movement is usually in time to music. People dance all over the world and in lots of different ways!

Let's party!
Dancing often happens when people get together, especially at celebrations like weddings and birthday parties. It helps a group share a special moment. Some dances may follow patterns and steps, others may just be freestyle.

What a performance!
Dance becomes more structured when it is performed. It usually has carefully planned steps, or choreography (see page 18). Dance theatre, such as a ballet or classical Indian dance, tells stories and expresses emotions.

Pop-video routines interpret the music with a huge variety of steps. The rules are not as strict as in classical dance.

WHOOPEE!

TA DAH!

Dance skills

At the highest levels, dancers learn great skills and train like athletes. Some dance has become a competitive sport, from ballroom dancing to hip-hop dance-offs and ice dancing.

GREAT FOOTWORK!

TIMING WAS A LITTLE OFF.

TOP MARKS FOR INTERPRETATION!

9   7   10

In all these dance sports, value is given to dancers' skills, but also the artistic element of the performance – how dancers interpret the music and communicate their feelings to the audience. This is central to the art of dance.

Do you want to find out more about the art of dance? The best way to do that is by asking questions, so let's get started!

Did cave people waltz?

No, the Stone-Age cave dwellers of thousands of years ago did not waltz. The waltz was only invented about 250 years ago. But we DO know our ancient ancestors danced, as they left cave paintings behind to show it.

NO THANKS!

LET'S ALL DO THE STONE-AGE CONGA!

Dancing on the wall

The earliest people boogied, possibly even before they spoke words to each other, and definitely before they wrote anything down! The Bhimbetka rock paintings in central India, showing people dancing in groups, date from over 10,000 years ago.

Dance into a trance

The oldest forms of dance are linked to storytelling – a way of passing on important history and beliefs. Dance also became part of religious rituals. In some cultures, people believe that dancing themselves into a trance-like state takes them closer to the spirit world or gods.

A Sufi Muslim group, Whirling Dervishes, spin to forget themselves and focus on God.

Ancient theatre
The ancient Greeks (around 1200 BCE–350 CE) painted dance scenes on their pottery, often linked to parties. Dances were performed in their theatres too, as part of a religious festival celebrating the Greek god Dionysus.

Changing styles
Dance styles have evolved over time. The waltz emerged in 18th-century Austria from a long tradition of dances to a 3-step rhythm (think oom-pah-pah, or 1,2,3; 1,2,3). This popular dance shocked some people at first, because couples danced so close together!

Ancient roots
The style of dancing that we see in Indian Bollywood films today has its roots in the ancient dances that told the stories of Hindu scriptures (holy texts).

Where do swords dance?

All over the world – from Scotland to Japan! All these dances probably developed for similar reasons: to call for strength before a battle or to celebrate a victory. But they are each linked to their own traditions.

The Scottish crossed-sword dance dates back over 600 years.

Japanese Samurai warriors practised their sword-handling skills in traditional dances.

Local roots

Almost every country and even region has folk dances. These are passed down the generations, with children learning the steps from their parents. Dancers wear traditional clothing and often perform at local celebrations or festivals.

In New Zealand, some Haka warrior dances are performed with long clubs.

The dancers at Salvador Carnival in Brazil express the country's mix of cultures, including its native population, descendants of Portuguese invaders and Africans who were forced there by the transatlantic slave trade.

Global growth

Over time, dances have adapted to the changing circumstances of the people who dance them. Migration has taken dances to other parts of the world, where they have mixed with existing traditions to create new ones.

Watch me move

Today, dance travels all over the world on our screens. New local dances emerge from the global mix. Those dances then spread out and become popular around the world.

Kizomba is an Angolan dance that has developed through lots of different influences. Today, it is popular across the globe thanks to social media.

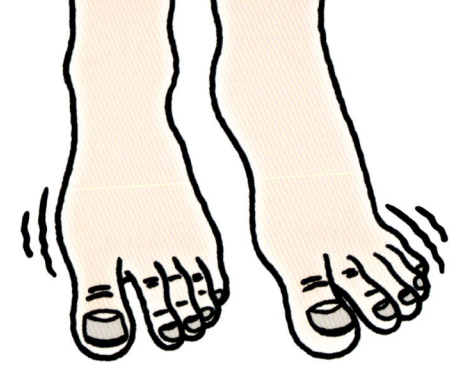

Can you have two left feet?

No, of course not! We use this expression to describe an awkward dancer. While some people can dance better than others, anyone can move to music – it's part of what makes us human.

Why we dance
Scientists think humans developed dance to help communication. It built group bonds and shared feelings. It also helped us to find a mate. Dancing today is still linked to dating and making friends.

Let it all out!
Humans also dance to be active, have fun and relax. It allows us to express feelings without words, and to enjoy moving our bodies. Better still, when we dance, our brain produces chemicals that make us happy!

Everyone can enjoy dancing, however they move.

Inbuilt ability

Humans respond to rhythm and music naturally. From around five months, babies begin to clap along or move their bodies in time to music. As we grow up, this natural ability is developed by watching family and friends, but also through dance lessons.

In control of your body

Dancing is all about controlling your body and making it move in particular way at a particular time. Dance lessons teach you steps and moves, as well as building strength and muscle control. Lessons improve your sense of rhythm and understanding of music, too.

How do you move to the groove?

By moving in time to the sound we are dancing to! This sound is usually music. In pop and jazz music, the word 'groove' can be used to describe the rhythm of a piece.

South African gumboot dancers do not use music. They create their own rhythm — and music — with the sound of their steps and claps!

Listen to the music

Like dance, music is a way humans communicate, but it is not visual, it is aural (something we hear). Music is a pattern of sounds we call notes. These notes can be high or low, soft or loud, long or short. The pattern often forms a melody, or tune.

Feel the beat!

Most music has a beat, a repeating pulse. The length of a beat gives music its timing, or tempo. Beats are grouped into bars. Each bar has particular number of beats, which usually stays the same, but number of notes may vary (as well as their length) and this gives music its rhythm.

The tempo of this Jewish wedding dance, called a Hora, gets faster and faster – and so does the dancing!

The swinging 1920s

Dance to the rhythm

Beat, rhythm and melody all come together to create a particular style of music. People usually dance to music with a regular beat and strong rhythm, because this helps us move in time to it.

The Charleston, a 1920s jazz dance, is usually danced to music with a four-beat bar that has three notes within it: two longer ones, followed by a short one. This breaks up the beat, giving the dance a quirky feel. Josephine Baker (1906–1975) helped make the Charleston popular.

When do people flap like a bird?

When they dance the Chicken Dance! The music was written by a Swiss accordion player in the 1950s. At some point, someone added chicken-like dance moves. In the 1980s, a hit record spread the dance around the world.

Shall we dance?
The Chicken Dance is silly and fun – perfect for everyone! Dances catch on and spread for lots of reasons – for example, a catchy tune, a driving rhythm or easy steps we can all follow.

CAN'T WAIT TO PLAY ROCK 'N' ROLL!

Mobile music
During the 19th century, it became much easier to print sheet music. Dances spread far and wide, as anyone who could read music could play tunes people liked dancing to. Then, the record player was invented – and the music industry exploded! Records could be played in the home or on a juke box. The era of popular music had begun.

Dance crazes

The birth of the music industry led to the spread of many dance styles and crazes. Jiving became popular in the 1930s. In the 1950s, rock 'n' roll and the twist took off. Other dance styles followed, from breakdancing to flossing.

Rock 'n' roll

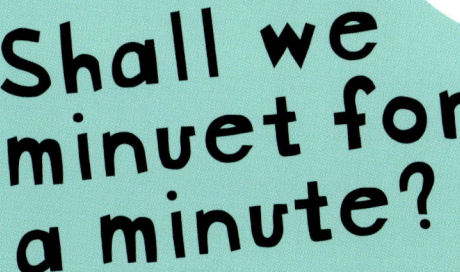

The twist

Breakdancing, or breaking

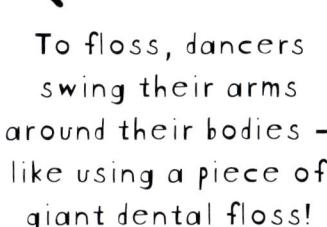

To floss, dancers swing their arms around their bodies — like using a piece of giant dental floss!

Shall we minuet for a minute?

In the 17th and 18th centuries, the minuet dance craze spread through the ballrooms of Europe from France. It was a slow, stately dance to music with a three-beats-in-a-bar rhythm. Its most spectacular versions were danced in the French royal court.

ONE, TWO, THREE — ONE, TWO, THREE...

Can you kick a can-can?

Possibly – if you are good at high kicks! The can-can is a type of dance that first became popular in the music halls of 19th-century France. Dancers showed off their skills with high-kicking, high-energy performances.

Putting on a show

Dance changes when it is a performance, as dancers entertain the audience by showing off their skills. Theatrical dance has ancient roots. Classical traditions in China and India date back over 2,000 years (see page 22), ballet over 1,500 years (see page 20). Dance is also often part of other performances, such as opera and musical theatre.

The opera *Carmen* often features choreography in the style of traditional Spanish dances, such as flamenco.

Spectacular staging

From the earliest times, dance shows wowed audiences with difficult steps and acrobatic moves. Dancers even flew in from the sides on wires! The theatre design helped, too. Pits or screens hid musicians, so the audience focused on the dancing.

Broadway melody

From the late 19th century, musical theatre was linked with Broadway, the theatre district of New York. Cinema took these song and dance shows around the world. Dancers performing in large groups, completely filling the stage (or screen), became central to a musical's wow factor.

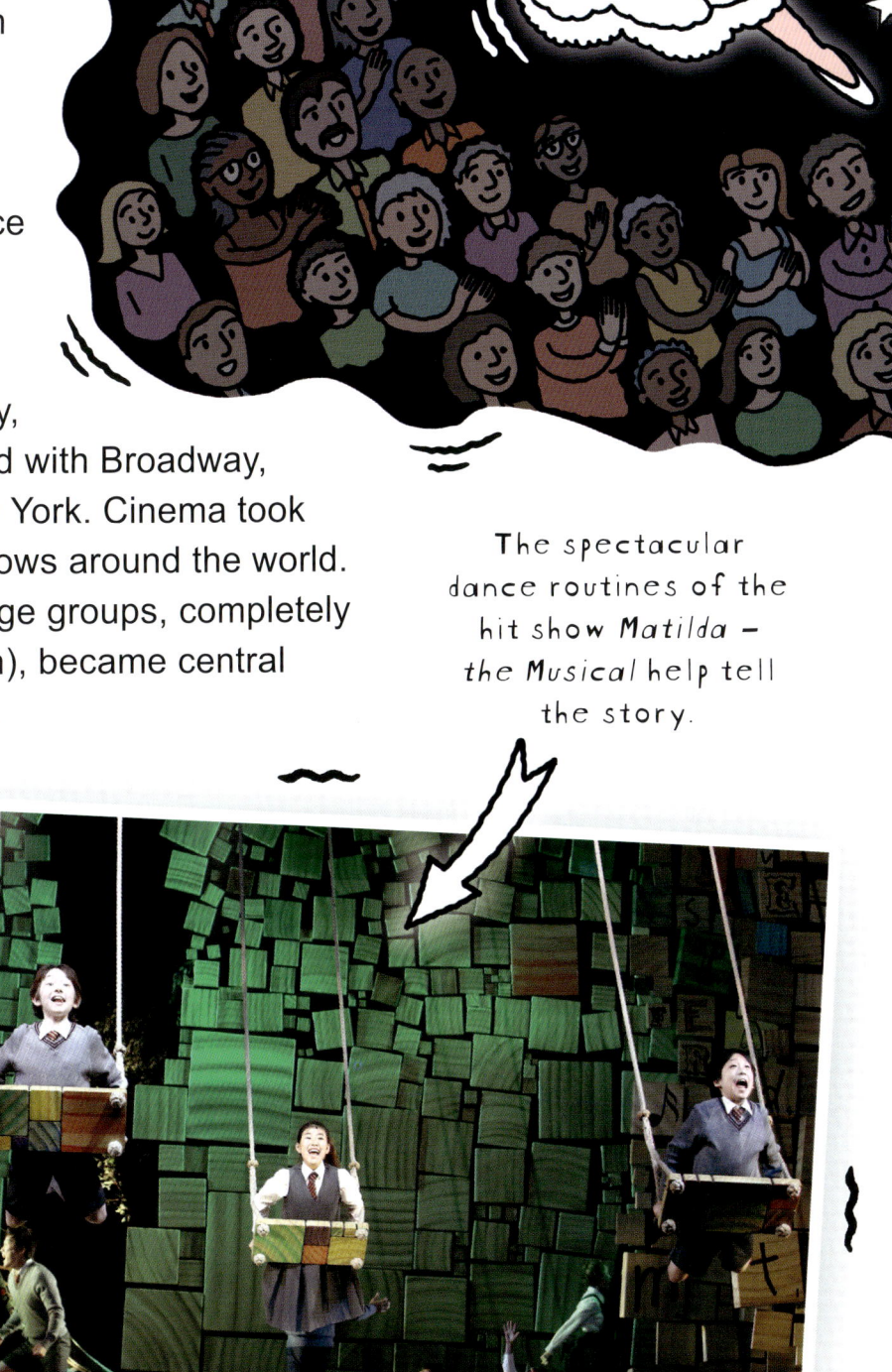

The spectacular dance routines of the hit show *Matilda – the Musical* help tell the story.

What puts the fizz into K-pop?

The dance routines! The music is great, of course, but it is the intricate, synchronised dance moves of the bands, that have made fizzy K-pop world-famous.

Dance writing

The word 'choreography' comes from the Greek for 'dance writing'. Most dance performances, from K pop to ballet, will have choreographers. They develop moves and how they are combined on stage.

Dances can be written down in different notations. They are often linked to musical notation, and describe the dancers' movements, as well as where they should be on stage.

18

An ancient art

Ancient dance shows had choreographers as well, but we only know a few of their names. The Emperor Xuanzong of China (685–763 CE) was famous for his love of dancing. He encouraged performances and choreographed several dances of his own.

LOOK! MY FEATHERS DANCE, TOO.

Xuanzong created the Rainbow Coat and Feathered Skirt dance for his wife, Yang Yuhuan.

From dancer to choreographer

Most choreographers trained as dancers and were successful performers before turning to choreography.

American Alvin Ailey (1931–1989) mixed ballet with modern dance and African-American dance traditions in his famous show *Revelations*.

Indian Geeta Kapur (1973–) learnt her craft while she was a dancer in Bollywood films. Today she is known as a judge in TV dance competitions.

Japanese-Filipino Rie Hata (1990–) is known as the 'Queen of Swag' for the signature style she developed as a dancer. This features in her choreography for Korean, Japanese and American pop groups.

What's the point of going en pointe?

To show off your amazing ballet skills! The dancer stands vertically on their toes with the help of special shoes. Pointe shoes are stiff and have a flat surface at the front end on which the dancer balances.

Strictly classical

Classical ballet has its roots in Italy, but became established as a dance form in the royal court of France in the 16th century. At first, even the king and queen took part. But, by the 19th century, it had developed into a highly technical art, performed by top professionals around Europe.

I'M THE KING OF BALLET!

French King Louis XIV (1638–1715) created and performed his own ballets.

Music and movement

Ballets often become as famous for their music as for their choreography. Orchestras will perform ballet music with no dancers at all. But for lovers of ballet, the magic is complete when it is combined with dance.

The ballet boss

Ballet masters and mistresses work with a group, or company, of dancers, making sure they do the steps correctly, train hard and interpret the music beautifully. Jules Perrot (1810–1892) and Marius Pepita (1819–1910) were both ballet masters for the Russian Imperial Ballet company. They are famous for their choreography, which is often still used.

In *The Dance Class*, French artist Edgar Degas (1834–1917) shows Jules Perrot, with his stick, instructing a group of dancers.

GOAT!

Ballet dancers are famous for their discipline and dedication to their art. Ballet fans argue about who are and who were the greatest ballet dancers.

Polish-Russian Vaslav Nijinsky (1890–1950) was celebrated for his great leaps and amazing technical skill. Unusually for a man, he could dance *en pointe*.

British Margot Fonteyn (1919–1991) and Russian Rudolph Nureyev (1938–1993) were one of the greatest ballet couples.

Misty Copeland (1982–) was one of the first African American ballerinas to become a lead dancer, when she performed in *The Firebird*.

When do you dance with your hands?

Nearly all the time! Dancing is about moving the whole body. Hands and arms can move in rhythm, just like feet, and they can be very expressive. In ballet and many Asian classical dance styles, hands are important for telling stories.

Sign language

Indian classical dance has different styles. Most tell religious stories and, as well as steps, use facial expressions and hand gestures, called *hasta mudras*. These add detail and emotion. Each hasta mudra has a name, and often more than one meaning.

Here are three hasta mudras and some of their meanings:

Sarpashirsha (snake head) Can represent being slow

Kartarimukh (scissor face) Can represent separation or death

Anjali (offering or greeting) One of many two-handed gestures

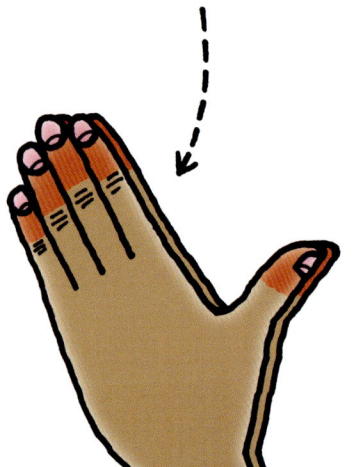

This dancer is using a hasta mudra in the **Odissi** dance tradition from eastern India.

Dances of devotion

Indian classical dance is first recorded around 200 BCE as part of Hindu religious rituals. Dancers use their whole body to celebrate their faith. They train for many years to perfect their movements.

In the **Kathak** tradition of northern India, dancers add to the music's rhythm with bells around their ankles.

Hands up!

Other dance traditions in Asia use dramatic hand gestures as part of their dances. They also have amazing costumes and tell exciting stories.

Some of the dances from the Indonesian island of Bali tell of mythical fights between Rangda, a demon queen, and Barong, a panther-like leader of good.

JINGLE! JINGLE!

LET'S HAVE A DANCE-OFF!

Barong

Rangda

How does a fox trot?

On four legs! But humans foxtrot on two. The foxtrot is a popular dance invented in the early 20th century in America. With its common 4-step rhythm, it can be danced to lots of different types of music.

Dance sport

The foxtrot has various different styles. The 'Slow Foxtrot' is one of the five standard ballroom dances recognised by the World DanceSport Federation (WDSF). This organisation sets the rules and oversees many dance competitions around the world, including para dance sport, disco and breakdancing.

Dancing together

In the ballroom dances, couple dance together in a 'closed position' – always in each other's arms. Dressed for a ball, they swirl elegantly around the floor.

Slow Foxtrot A steady, gliding foxtrot

Other standard ballroom dances include:

Viennese Waltz The original, fast waltz

Waltz A slow 'English' waltz

Tango An adapted version of the Argentine tango

Quickstep Fast and fun, evolving from the foxtrot and Charleston

Dancing apart

The other WDSF standard dances are grouped as 'Latin', as they are often danced to Spanish and South American rhythms. Couples dance together but not always in a closed position. These dances focus on hip movement.

Paso Doble
A fast Spanish dance, linked to bullfighting

Other Latin dances include:

Rumba
A US dance inspired by a Cuban one

Cha-cha-cha
A Cuban dance inspired by music of the same name

Samba
Originating in Brazil, a dance with a rise-and-fall movement

Jive
An African-American dance linked to swing

Strictly ballroom

Modern ballroom dances emerged in the early to mid-20th century, and TV competitions have made them popular again. The British show *Strictly Come Dancing* was first broadcast in 2004. Variations of the show, usually called *Dancing with the Stars*, are now made in 60 other countries.

The TV format pairs celebrities with professional dancers. It shows how hard dancers work, but also that anyone can learn to dance.

How can dance break all the rules?

Easily! We can all dance and twirl without following set steps. Since the 1960s, it has become much more common to dance on your own or in a group, rather than as a couple. But even in formal dancing, things have moved on.

Free dance

In the late 19th century, some classically trained ballet dancers began to break the rules. They no longer danced *en pointe* and moved more naturally, improvising their movements. This became known as free dance.

American dancer and choreographer Isadora Duncan (1877–1927) pioneered free dance, amazing audiences with the beauty of her style and shocking them with her bare feet.

Dancing today

Free dance led to styles such as modern and contemporary. These take their influences from many places – from jazz and pop music to traditional dances from all around the world. Dancers train just as hard as they do in classical traditions, but use a much broader range of movement.

Choreographer Matthew Bourne (1960–) combined contemporary styles with classical ballet music in his production of *Swan Lake*. All the swans were danced by men, rather than women.

Jazz dance styles, strongly influenced by African-American dance traditions, are found in just about every type of modern dance.

Express yourself!

Martha Graham (1894–1991), a modern dancer and teacher, famously said: **"Dance is the hidden language of the soul."** Whether dancing on our own or in a group, to set steps or freestyle, dance is a universal way of expressing our feelings.

Let's dance!

Quick-fire questions

ROAR!

When do eyebrows dance?

In some Indian classical dancing! Eyebrow movement can be a form of sign language. In Kathak dancing, 'Chatura' is where both eyebrows are raised and lowered quickly. It can mean joy or excitement.

When do lions dance?

At Chinese New Year. This traditional Chinese dance is usually performed by two dancers dressed as a lion. Its steps are linked to Chinese martial arts.

Which one-hit wonder sparked a dance craze?

Macarena, a dance remix of a Flamenco song, by Los Del Rio. It unexpectedly sparked a global dance craze in 1996 with its video, which featured easy-to-follow steps. It still gets played at weddings today!

Which type of dance does a 'horse step'?

Ballet! The language of classical ballet is French, and often describes steps and movements using animals or objects. In a *pas de cheval*, the dancer points one foot, stretches the leg out – lowers it to the ground, and pulls it towards the standing leg, a little like a horse pawing the ground. Here are a few others:

Sissonne
'Scissor-like'
A jump during which the outstretched legs are separated and then brought back together again, like scissor blades.

Pas de chat
'Step of the cat'
A sideways jump that pulls up both knees, trying to imitate a leaping cat.

Cloche
'Bell'
Moving one leg to the front and then the back, off the floor, again and again, like a bell swinging back and forth.

Can you conga in Cuba?

Yes! The conga is based on a Cuban street dance with African origins. With three simple steps, the human-chain dance is now popular all over the world. The longest ever conga line was made up of 119,986 people in Miami, USA, in 1988.

Glossary

Ballroom dance Originally a term for formal dances, now used to describe the dance sport, performed in pairs.

Bar In music, a group of beats. Each bar usually contains the same number of beats, creating the music's rhythm.

Beat A regular pulse, like a heartbeat, of a piece of music.

Bollywood The informal name used to describe India's film industry.

Choreography The planned sequence of steps in a dance, or the art of creating this sequence. A person who designs these steps is called a choreographer.

Classical Describes formal music and dance traditions that have a long history.

Contemporary dance A style of dance that emerged in the 20th century. It mixes many styles and traditions.

Dance notation A graphic or written record of dance steps and movements.

Free dance A dance style that emerged in the late 19th century, often responding to the music instantly rather than planning steps in advance.

Haka A variety of formal, traditional dances of the Māori people of New Zealand.

Hip-hop A style of music and dance, with strong rhythms and beat, that developed in African-American culture in the 1980s.

Jazz A type of music that developed from African-American culture in the early 20th century.

Jazz dance A dance style that began from dances linked to jazz music, but was developed by choreographers for musical theatre and film.

Latin In dance and music, describes styles or traditions linked to Spain, Portugal or Central and South America.

Modern dance A style of dance that does not follow the strict rules of ballet.

Music hall A kind of theatre that staged variety entertainment. This included singing, dancing, comedy and acrobatics.

Rhythm A pattern of musical notes of varying length built around the music's beat.

Samurai A member of a once powerful group of elite soldiers in Japan.

Tempo The speed a piece of music is played at.

Waltz A dance performed to a three-beat rhythm that originated in Austria. There are several different styles of waltz.

Further discovery

You can enjoy dance just by watching it on the Web, from ballet to recent pop videos. If you can, try to see a live dance performance, too. And, of course, you can always dance – perhaps take some lessons. The links and books here might inspire you!

Websites

kids.kiddle.co/Dance
A brief overview of dance with a lot of useful links to particular dance styles and some famous dancers.

youtube.com/watch?v=52bscmW8x8O
A performance of an Odissi dance, using hasta mudras (see page 22). The dance starts about 50 seconds into the clip.

bbc.co.uk/programmes/b00q9n6d/clips
A BBC selection that showcases a selection of dances from around the world.

Books

Anything is Possible with Ballet
by Steven McCrae (Magic Cat, 2025)

Musicals: The Definitive Illustrated Story
by DK, foreword by Elaine Page (Dorling Kindersley, 2021)

Get Active: Dance
by Alix Wood (Wayland, 2020)

Welcome to the Arts: Dance
by Sir Alastair Spalding (Big Picture Press, 2023)

Every effort has been made by the Publishers to ensure that the websites in this book are suitable for children, that they are of the highest educational value, and that they contain no inappropriate or offensive material. However, because of the nature of the Internet, it is impossible to guarantee that the contents of these sites will not be altered. We strongly advise that Internet access is supervised by a responsible adult.

Index

A
Ailey, Alvin 19
ancient China 19
ancient Greece 7

B
Baker, Josephine 13
ballet 4, 16, 18–22, 26–27, 29
ballroom dance 5, 24–25
beat 13, 15
Bhimbetka rock paintings 6
Bollywood 7, 19
Bourne, Matthew 27
breakdancing *see* breaking
breaking 15, 24
Broadway 17

C
Carmen 16
carnival, Brazil 9
cave people 6
cha-cha-cha 25
Charleston 13, 24
Chicken Dance 14
Chinese dance, traditional 16, 19, 28
choreography 4, 16, 18–21
choreographers 18–21, 26–27
classical dance 4–5, 16, 20, 22–23, 26–29
conga 29
contemporary (dance) 27
Copeland, Misty 21

D
dance crazes 15, 28
Duncan, Isadora 26

E
en pointe (ballet) 20–21, 26

F
floss (dance) 15
Fonteyn, Margot 21
foxtrot 24
free dance 26–27
freestyle 4, 27

G
Graham, Martha 27
gumboot dance 12

H
Haka warrior dance 8
hasta mudras 22
Hata, Rie 19
hip-hop 5
Hora 13

I
ice dance 5
Indian dance, classical 4, 7, 16, 22–23, 28
Indonesian dance, traditional 23

J
jazz dance 13, 26
jazz music 12, 26
jive 15, 25

K
Kapur, Geeta 19
Kathak dance tradition 23, 28
Kizomba 9
K-pop 18–19

L
lessons, dance 11
lion dance 28

M
Matilda – The Musical 17
minuet 15
modern (dance) 19, 27
musical theatre 16–17

N
Nijinsky, Vaslav 21
notation (choreography) 18
Nureyev, Rudolph 21

O
Odissi dance tradition 22
opera 16

P
paso doble 25
Pepita, Marius 21
Perrot, Jules 21
pointe shoes 20
pop music 5, 12, 27

Q
quickstep 24

R
Rainbow Coat and Feathered Skirt dance 19
Revelations 19
rhythm 7, 11–15, 22–25
rock 'n' roll 15
rumba 25

S
samba 25
Samurai 8

T
tango 24
TV dance shows 19, 25
twist (dance) 15

W
waltz 6–7, 24
Whirling Dervishes 6

A Question of the Arts titles:

978 1 5263 2975 2
978 1 5263 2976 9

What is architecture?
Who was the first architect?
Why doesn't a building fall down?
Did the little pigs build with poo?
Can you ever have enough turrets?
When is an onion a roof?
Why are architects copycats?
Can brutal be beautiful?
Why try to scrape the sky?
Can you fit over 100,000
bottoms on seats?
Can a building fry an egg?
Will future homes be hobbit houses?

978 1 5263 2985 1
978 1 5263 2986 8

What is craft?
Did a potter reinvent the wheel?
Can you blow bubbles with … glass?
How do you make a leaf out of gold?
How can an egg
be worth a million pounds?
How do you spin a wooden leg?
What hot dog can you sit on?
How do you make a woolly jumper?
Who was a jean genius?
Were handbags big in the Stone Age?
Can you make paper from sunflowers?
Is the future of craft rubbish?

978 1 5263 2977 6
978 1 5263 2978 3

What is dance?
Did cave people waltz?
Where do swords dance?
Can you have two left feet?
How do you move to the groove?
When do people flap like a bird?
Can you kick a can-can?
What puts the fizz into K-pop?
What's the point of going *en pointe*?
When do you dance with your hands?
How does a fox trot?
How can dance break all the rules?

978 1 5263 2983 7
978 1 5263 2984 4

What is film?
How did cinema begin with a bad joke?
When do cowboys eat spaghetti?
How did Snow White become
a film star?
What makes an elevator pitch?
Who are film's action stars?
What makes a film star shine?
Why did ET cut Indiana Jones?
Is the force with you?
When was a dog's life a surprise hit?
Is an Oscar named after
somebody's bottom?
Will the big screen become
the small screen?

978 1 5263 2980 6
978 1 5263 2981 3

What is fine art?
Who were the first artists
Is art history?
When does a dot go for a walk?
When does art enter
another dimension?
Can you print a masterpiece?
How can you make art in a snap?
What made the Mona Lisa smile?
When do artists paint haystacks?
When is a bowl of fruit a face?
When is a lobster a telephone?
Why is art's future confused?

978 1 5263 2987 5
978 1 5263 2988 2

What is literature?
Why do we care about old books?
What makes legends legendary?
When is poetry free?
Can a pop star be a poet?
Does a play need an audience?
What's the art of windmill fighting?
Was Frankenstein really a monster?
Is life just a dream?
When is a dog a writer?
Are fairy tales a bit … grim?
Can monkeys write novels?

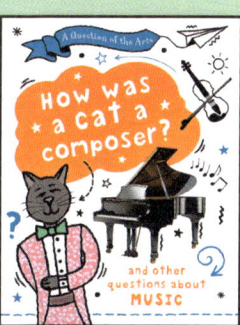

978 1 5263 2989 9
978 1 5263 2990 5

What is music?
When is a song like a worm?
How does a boom bap make you hip hop?
Can a lightning bolt make music?
Can you sing a solo duet?
What makes a fab four?
Who waves a wand to make music?
How did a cat become a composer?
Who played an upside-down guitar?
When does music bring the
house down?
How does a chip become a tune?
Will computers replace composers?

978 1 5263 2979 0
978 1 5263 2982 0

What is theatre?
Why did ancient Greeks
throw food at actors?
Who put on the first Christmas show?
Can it rain in the theatre?
Why do some plays end in tears?
What's so funny about a comedy?
Can a play have no actors?
When is a lion the star of the show?
Why is Shakespeare the G.O.A.T.?
When does a boy act a girl acting a boy?
How is it always all right on the night?
Will the show go on?